Gourmet Embellishments

with Metallic Threads & Fibers

An  In Cahoots® embellishment workbook
by Debbie Garbers and Janet F. O'Brien

Gourmet Embellishments with Metallic Threads

Copyright © 1996, 1997 ⚜ In Cahoots®
ISBN 0-9653079-1-3
First Edition
All rights reserved
Published in Roswell, Georgia
In Cahoots
P O Box 72336
Marietta, GA 30007-2336 USA
770-641-0945

We have worked hard to make this book accurate, complete, and easy to follow. However, In Cahoots cannot guarantee results since selection of supplies and products vary. No warranty is implied, and In Cahoots assumes no responsibility for use of this information.

Product descriptions in this book are from the best available information in the spring of 1997. Of course, manufacturers constantly expand and change their product lines, so check with your dealer for availability.

Fibers and other products vary widely in availability and quality. Whenever specific brand names are mentioned, it usually means the authors have used the products and were pleased with the results. If you're having trouble using a product that is not listed in this workbook, try one of the products listed in this book to make sure the problem is not with your machine or sewing technique.

The use of brand names in this guide is also intended to save readers time. There may be other products that are comparable. Be sure to test with the exact project materials, especially when working with unfamiliar fabrics, threads, and fibers.

Teachers have permission to use this book to teach classes as long as each student purchases a personal copy of the book.

Stitch samples used in this book were stitched on the following machines: Bernina 1530 & 930, Pfaff 7550 & 7570, and Viking # 1.

Images used in this book are protected by copyright by the following copyright holders: Corel Corporation, In Cahoots.

⚜

Printed in the United States of America.

⚜

About the Authors

Debbie Garbers and Janet O'Brien are garment designers, authors, and teachers with a special interest in embellishment, textures, fibers, and colors. They believe art-to-wear clothing should enhance the wearer and satisfy the creative sewer. Their philosophy carries over to their teaching and writing. They develop classes and patterns so the average sewer can enjoy creating her own artful garments and accessories.

Debbie and Janet met about six years ago in a surface design class. They both had learned sewing and needlecrafts as children and were looking for new ways to use their sewing machines. They kept bumping into each other in classes and meetings where they shared information and their sewing enthusiasm.

When Debbie and Janet began teaching together in 1993, they saw the need for flattering art-to-wear patterns with thorough directions. As a result, they started In Cahoots to fill this void. They now have six garment patterns that include embellishment, piecing, and pin weaving techniques. All of the patterns are classroom tested before production, and all include thorough instructions with clear drawings. The embellished vest patterns have helpful information about decorative threads as well as detailed machine set-up directions for each technique.

They publish the best selling book, *Point Well Taken, The Guide to Success with Needles & Threads* and have a series of workbooks for learning about stitches, threads, fibers, and needles. This book, *Gourmet Embellishments with Metallic Threads*, is the first in that series.

Patterns and books are available at local quilt and sewing shops or directly from In Cahoots.

Internationally recognized for their garment designs, Debbie and Janet have an ensemble in the '96 - '97 Fairfield Fashion Show and have been invited to participate in the '97 - '98 show. They both have had ensembles in the American Quilter's Society Fashion Show, Mid-Atlantic Wearable Art Festival, Pennsylvania National Quilt Extravaganza, and the Pacific International Festival. Janet won first place ribbons for ensembles in the '96 Pacific International Festival and the *Sewing with Nancy Challenge*. Debbie has had vests in the Hoffman Challenge Exhibits, and they have a vest and instructions in the Sulky book, *Embellishing Concepts in Sulky*.

Acknowledgments

After teaching consumers, shop owners, and shop teachers about needles and threads over the past five years, we have finally condensed our "teaching notes" in a series of workbooks. It was the encouragement from our students that made us even consider such an undertaking. Since we want our students to spend their class time sewing and experimenting, not taking notes, we designed this workbook format to include lots of room for samples.

We'd like to thank our mothers, grandmothers, and aunts, who helped us learn how to sew. We'd also like to thank the teachers who have shared their knowledge of sewing with us.

Without the support of our families, this book would have been impossible. Thank you — Jeff, Kathy, Ray, Betty, Jason, Jim, Alison, Laverne, Tom, and Debbie. Of all the people who've helped us in this endeavor, we'd like to offer a special thanks to our web site designer, illustrator, editor, and computer wizard, Jeff Garbers.

Thank you also to our "beta testers", Helena Krapp, Alice Crawford, Carol Britt, and the students at Sew What Fabrics in Wytheville, Virginia.

Trademarks and Brand Names Used in This Book

We have made every attempt to properly credit the trademarks and brand names listed in this book. We apologize for any that are not listed correctly.

Berol® Dental Floss Threader is a registered trademark of Gum
Creative Feet™ is a trademark of Creative Feet
Easy Tear™ is a trademark of Graphic Impressions
In Cahoots® and the ⚓ logo are registered trademarks of In Cahoots
Madeira® is a registered trademark of Madeira Threads (UK) Ltd.
Pearls & Piping™ is a trademark of Creative Feet
Pigma Micron is a brand name of Sakura Color Products Corp., Japan
Satin Edge™ is a trademark of Creative Feet
Schmetz is a brand name of Ferd. Schmetz GmbH, Germany
Sequins & Ribbon™ is a trademark of Creative Feet
Sewers Aid is a brand name of W. H. Collins, Inc.
Sharpie® Ultra Fine Point is a registered trademark of Sanford®
Spool Tool™ is a trademark of Master Piece®
Stitch and Ditch™ is a trademark of Thread Pro
Stitch and Ditch Heirloom™ is a trademark of Thread Pro
Stitch and Tear™ is a trademark of Fredenberg Nonwovens, Pellon® Division
Sulky® is a registered trademark of Sulky of America
Tear-Away is a brand name of Sew Art Internatioal
Thread Pro™ is a trademark of Thread Pro
Thread-Wrap® is a registered trademark of Katie Lane
Totally Stable is a brand name of Sulky of America
Ultrasuede® and Ultrasuede Light® are registered trademarks of Springs Industries
Dental Floss Threader is a registered trademark of Gum

Books in This Series:

- Gourmet Embellishments with Metallic Threads & Fibers

- Decorative Pizzazz You Can Do Without a Fancy Machine

- Two Needles Are Better Than One

- Uncommon Threads, Uncommon Results

Table Of Contents

Introduction

Machine embellishment is an exciting extension of our sewing and needlework experiences. But there are so many embellishment options today. Where does one begin? We faced the same question when we began teaching machine embellishment classes over five years ago.

This series of classes and resulting workbooks evolved from our quest for a systematic way to teach machine embellishment. Our goal was to write instructions that are clear and thorough, so that all readers might develop their stitching skills and gain confidence in them. *Gourmet Embellishments with Metallic Threads and Fibers* includes specific exercises using metallic threads, mylar threads, couching fibers, and trims.

We wrote *Gourmet Embellishments* with many readers in mind:

- Stitchers who are new to embellishment and may be a little intimidated by it.

- Stitchers who have tried embellishment but didn't get the results they were expecting.

- Stitchers with some embellishment experience who want some new stitching techniques or new embellishment resources.

- Stitchers who consider themselves dabblers and enjoy the challenge of learning.

- Teachers who want a workbook for their students to use in embellishment classes.

- Students who will use this book as a guide in their embellishment classes or independent study.

Gourmet Embellishments contains a series of embellishment exercises that will help you explore techniques, needles, metallic threads, fibers, and related supplies. While stitching, you will learn to take full advantage of your machine even if you think it is very limited. As a result, you will become much better acquainted with your machine. In addition, this book includes tips to help you improve and simplify your stitching.

If you want to know more about needles, threads, or other products for embellishment projects, you'll enjoy our reference book *Point Well Taken: The Guide to Success with Needles & Threads*. We encourage you to learn hands-on use of decorative threads and special purpose needles. For more exciting projects we suggest trying our patterns: *Moonstruck* for the beginning embellisher, *Great Squares* for the confident beginner, and *Sheer Illusions* for the intermediate stitcher.

We wrote *Gourmet Embellishments* for you to develop and expand your embellishment repertoire, but we encourage you to use it as a springboard to become an adventurous, creative, and satisfied stitcher. No matter what experiences you bring to this book, our goal is to help you build a stitch journal of techniques upon which to draw in the future. Using your stitch journal, you can begin to match stitch design, thread, and texture to fabric and layout. You are about to begin an exciting journey. Relax, and enjoy stitching!

How to Use This Book

The ideal way to use this workbook is to begin with the first exercise and work through all the exercises. However, we know our readers have many different machine embellishment skills, experiences, interests, and goals, so we recommend that you first take a few minutes to look over this book to determine your path.

As you preview this workbook, you will notice that the exercises contain illustrations, step by step directions, very specific machine set-up information, and places for you to fill in settings you find are best with your machine. We included this detailed information for several reasons. First, it is reassuring to begin a new lesson having all the information needed to set up the machine. Second, the set-up charts and step-by-step recipe approach eliminate the need for guesswork when stitchers may not have all of the information or experience to know what choices have to be made. So, take the time to follow all of the directions carefully, and you should have success immediately.

How do you know if your stitches are of good quality? To determine good quality stitching, examine your sample from both the right and the wrong sides. Are the stitches uniform in size? Are you able to see only the needle thread on the right side of the fabric? If you can answer yes to these questions, then you have good quality stitching. Once you know the difference between good and poor quality stitching, you can decide when a "goof" is an exciting variation of a technique described in this workbook. Sometimes these decisions are a matter of personal taste or creativity.

Once you have been successful in reproducing the technique with good quality stitches, feel free to use the exercises as a jumping off point to add your own touch of creativity to your work. For example, although we wrote this book for metallic threads, you may use the techniques with rayon threads as well.

As you stitch, you will become more comfortable with embellishment as well as learning new techniques. Take the time to practice on stitch samples, even though it's tempting to try something new in a project. Experiment and "work the bugs out" ahead of time so you don't run into unexpected problems and ruin good fabric. The time you spend practicing will save time and reduce frustration later. You will also come to know and love your machine and accessories even more!

One final note: TAKE A BREAK ABOUT EVERY 45 MINUTES! It is too easy to stitch and lose all concept of time. This may be satisfying to your mind, but your body will not appreciate your intense concentration after a while. When you finally try to dislodge yourself from your chair, you will not be able to budge. So set your kitchen timer and take a stretch break at the end of a 45 minute period.

Tools and Supplies

Choosing the right tools and supplies is so important for your success in stitching with metallic threads and fibers or any other kind of sewing. You do not need a fancy sewing machine to explore the embellishment possibilities highlighted in this book, but you should begin your exploration with high quality supplies. Careful preparation will set the stage for many hours of creative fun and satisfaction.

Supply List

More information about the following supplies is given immediately following the supply list.

- ❏ Sewing machine in good working order
- ❏ Machine manual, accessories, and usual sewing supplies
- ❏ Paper, pencil, and highlighter for notes
- ❏ Three-ring binder & top loading plastic page protectors
- ❏ Ultra Fine Sharpie® marker or Micro Pigma pen
- ❏ 1 yd. 100 % cotton fabric in a light solid color
- ❏ 1 fat quarter 100 % cotton printed fabric with stripes
- ❏ 1 yd. stabilizer
- ❏ Schmetz Universal 80 / 12 Needle
- ❏ Schmetz Embroidery Needles size 75 / 11 or 90 / 14
- ❏ Schmetz Metallica or Lammertz Nadlen Metafil Needles size 80 / 12
- ❏ One empty bobbin
- ❏ White bobbin thread
- ❏ At least two different coordinating spools of metallic thread in a solid color
- ❏ At least one coordinating variegated spool of metallic thread
- ❏ One spool of mylar thread
- ❏ Couching fibers such as Candlelight, Glamour, Pearl Crown Rayon, and Pearl Cotton.
- ❏ **Optional Couching Fibers**: Designer Threads, On The Surface, Mulit's™ Embellishment Yarn, Bouclé, Chenille, Frappé, Radiance, and fibers from The Weaving Edge: Embellish It™, The Embellishing Bobbin™, and Textural Accents™
- ❏ Appliqué, embroidery, satin stitch, or zig zag foot
- ❏ Piping, beading, or braiding foot
- ❏ Couching, cording, and / or 3 to 9 hole cording foot
- ❏ **Highly recommended**: In Cahoots book *Point Well Taken*
- ❏ **Optional Feet**: Creative Feet: Pearls & Piping™, or Sequins & Ribbon™
- ❏ **Optional Products:** (For more information about these, see notes throughout the book and *Point Well Taken*)
  - ❏ Perfect Sew Needle Threader / Needle Inserter
  - ❏ Lube-A-Thread
  - ❏ monofilament thread
  - ❏ Multiple Cording Guide
  - ❏ Sewer's Aid
  - ❏ Spinster
  - ❏ Spool Tool™
  - ❏ Thread Palette
  - ❏ Thread Pro
  - ❏ Thread Twirler
  - ❏ Thread-Wrap®

Your Sewing Machine

A basic machine is all that you need to explore the embellishment possibilities covered in this book. The exercises use zig zag and utility stitches plus optional open and closed decorative stitch designs. You need only a few stitch choices to achieve spectacular and satisfying results. It is helpful to be able to override automatic stitch design settings. Check your machine manual for more specific information on stitch length and width settings.

Before changing any machine settings, make a note of the settings you use for regular sewing. Your notes will save you a lot of time later! Be sure to note any changes for future reference, also.

It is advantageous to use your machine table to keep fabric flat while stitching. If you do not have such a table or yours is too small to support your fabric adequately, you can purchase a table surface for your machine, such as a *Sew Steady Portable Table*. (See *Supply Sources*, page 42.)

You may also want to have additional lighting while sewing. A desk lamp such as the Ott light adds good lighting to the stitching area.

Machine Accessory Feet

You will usually use an appliqué, embroidery, satin stitch, or zig zag foot for the techniques covered in this book. These feet have a groove or channel on the bottom that allows them to glide smoothly over the heavy thread build up of wide satin and decorative stitches. Check the channel on the underside of the foot to make sure it is deep and wide enough for even stitching. Some appliqué feet are clear or have "open toes" that give a good view of the stitching path. If you experience problems with irregular stitch quality or with the machine feeding the fabric properly, try another foot to see if that solves the problem.

For the heavier fibers that are too thick to pass through the eye of the needle, you will be using several different types of accessory feet. These include cording, braiding, piping, beading, couching, and 3 to 9 hole cording feet. These feet have one or more grooves on the bottom that are deep and wide enough to ride smoothly over the heavier fibers. Match the thickness of the couching fibers to the depth of the foot groove for best results. For each exercise, we do list which foot is necessary. You may want to use a couching foot with a braiding guide or a *Multiple Cording Guide* to hold the yarn straight in front of the presser foot. See the *Glossary* (page 40) for more information.

If your machine did not come with these type of presser feet, you may be able to purchase accessory feet from your machine dealer. If none are available for your machine, you may be able to purchase generic accessory feet either from the dealer or through *Clotilde's or Nancy's Notion's* catalog. The *Creative Feet™* company makes several wonderful couching style feet that fit on nearly every machine. (See *Supply Sources*, page 42.)

Fabric

For creating your stitch samples, use a medium weight 100% cotton fabric that you have prewashed and ironed. Choose a light, solid color or muslin fabric. Use natural fiber fabrics for any type of embellishment projects. For the technique exercises in this book, we recommend that you cut 8" x 10" pieces of fabric, which fit well into the top loading page protectors you will use to store samples.

Threads

Investment in good quality thread pays off in sewing ease and beautiful stitches. There are many thread choices, but the best choice is a name brand thread of good quality. These threads are stronger and more lustrous than bargain varieties.

Needle Threads

Metallic threads reflect light for added dimension and sparkle. Check the thread before purchasing to make sure it doesn't feel stiff, as stiff threads won't easily pass through the needle. Choose metallic threads that give you enough "bang for your buck." Metallic thread that has a lot of white showing in addition to the color does not give as much of a metallic look when stitched. The white that shows is the core fiber that is blended with the metallic fibers. Choose threads that don't have a lot of the core showing and avoid metallics which tend to fray badly.

When stitching the exercises in this workbook, stick to a few solid and variegated colors that you like and that will show up on your fabric. Use a few colors at first until you are confident of your stitching, then try different kinds of metallics with the same stitch to compare the results. You don't need a big stash of thread to learn these techniques, but it is nice to have many threads and fibers to choose from when you "graduate" to specific projects.

Sulky and Madeira Metallic manufacture fine quality metallic threads that are good for learning. When you become adventurous, compare the special effects of Maderia Supertwist and FS Jewel. For more about threads, see *Point Well Taken*.

Mylar (or tinsel thread) is a flat, highly reflective, ribbon-like polyester thread. Embroidery designs take on a stunning luster when sewn with this flat thread. Because it is flat, it does not completely fill in satin stitches or embroidery motifs that contain satin stitch elements. It sews straight, utility, and open decorative stitches beautifully. The following mylar threads are suitable for the purposes of these exercises: *Sulky Sliver*, *Maderia Jewel*, and *Prizm* tinsel thread. Again, you do not need a stash of colors for this book.

TIP: Sew with the mylar spools in a vertical sewing position.

Couching Threads / Fibers / Trims

You ca use threads, fibers, and trims that are too large to go through the eye of the needle for embellishment. In this workbook, several couching techniques are covered. Metallic threads, monofilament threads and other decorative threads are suitable needle threads for couching. There are many heavier fibers that work well for couching. To learn the couching techniques in this book, choose *Candlelight*, *Glamour*, or any knitting yarns you may have on hand. Refer to the list of optional couching fibers on the supply list. Refer to the list of optional couching fibers on the supply list. Once you are confident of your skills in couching, turn to *Point Well Taken* for a comprehensive list and description of couching fibers available.

TIP: Use Thread-Wraps® or Thread Savers to keep decorative threads from unwinding in storage.

TIP: For couching eyelash yarns, use the blind hem stitch. Brush the eyelashes to the left of the main yarn cord. Stitch just to the right of the main cord so that the zig zag stitch catches this cord but not the eyelashes.

Bobbin Thread

For embellishment stitching, use a fine bobbin or lingerie thread in the bobbin. Regular sewing thread would build up on the wrong side of the fabric, causing the machine to jam and distort the fabric and stitches. Bobbin threads usually come in white or black only. Good choices include *YLI Lingerie & Bobbin Thread, Sew-Bob, Madeira Bobbinfil,* or *Sulky® Bobbin Thread.* For older machines that may have trouble sewing with the above threads, try *J & P Coats Dual Duty Plus® Extra Fine.* As a last resort, try regular polyester thread if the Coats fine thread doesn't solve the problem. For the technique exercises in this book, we recommend that you wind several bobbins before you start sewing.

NOTE: When using monofilament thread in the needle, use polyester sewing thread in the bobbin.

NOTE: Be sure to wind bobbin threads slowly, as they will stretch with high speed winding, resulting in puckered stitching.

Needles

Like thread, there are many choices of needles, but the best choice is a name brand needle of good quality. Investment in good quality needles and threads will reward you with sewing ease and satisfaction. For stitching with mylar threads, use a 75 / 11 embroidery needle or an 80 / 12 universal needle. For stitching with all other metallic threads, use an 80 / 12 metallica needle or a 90 / 14 embroidery needle.

Even the highest quality needle will dull, bend, or form burrs after stitching through fabric and stabilizer; so change your needle frequently. Become attuned to the normal stitching sound of your machine, so that you will immediately recognize the sound of a damaged needle or a machine that needs cleaning and oiling. A damaged needle will not only produce poor stitch quality, but it can also seriously damage the bobbin system. The best prevention is your alert response to needle damage. If your needle breaks, make sure you remove the bobbin and throat plate to clean out any tiny bit of metal before inserting a new needle. For more information and tips about needles, refer to *Point Well Taken.*

TIP: Store slightly-used needles in a tomato pincushion you have labeled with a Sharpie® marker.

TIP: To keep threads and fibers dust-free, keep them in a closed container. We do not recommend storing in a tightly-sealed plastic box, as threads need some air to "breathe." To protect threads on a thread rack, cover loosely with a piece of fabric.

Stabilizers

Stabilizers provide support to both the fabric and to the stitches themselves to eliminate puckered fabric and skipped or irregular stitches. They are placed under the wrong side of the fabric next to the throat plate, and all stitching is done through the fabric and stabilizer. Good choices include lightweight nonwoven stabilizers such as *Easy Tear™, Stitch & Ditch™, Stitch & Ditch Heirloom™, Sulky Tear Easy, Stitch & Tear, No Whiskers*, and *Tear Away Soft*. You may also use freezer paper, copier paper, or computer paper to stabilize your stitch samples. Because these are paper products, you will hear a slight popping noise as the needle pierces. Stitching through paper also dulls your needle faster than when sewing with the nonwovens mentioned above. For more information about other stabilizers available for projects, see *Point Well Taken* and In Cahoots patterns. For the technique exercises in this book, we recommend that you cut 8" x 9" pieces of stabilizer. This size fits well into the top loading page protectors we use to store samples.

Getting Started

Getting Your Machine Ready

Begin with a clean and oiled machine every time you sit down to sew. Threads, especially the decorative kind, throw off a lot of lint that collects under the throat plate and in the bobbin area. Follow your machine manual to clean these areas either with a brush or a bent pipe cleaner. Bend the pipe cleaner in half so you don't scratch your machine with the end of the wire. Put a drop of oil on a soft cotton swab and wipe around the bobbin area. Be careful to draw the lint out of the machine and not push it back further into the bobbin area. Draw the middle section of a pipe cleaner *gently* through the tension disks to clean out lint and stray bits of thread. You can also use special vacuum cleaner attachments to suck out lint. We do not recommend using canned air, as it blows lint and possibly condensation back into the machine.

Relieving Tension Headaches

To get good stitch quality, you will need to adjust your machine tension. To check for the correct tension, examine your work:

- The needle thread should be pulled slightly to the wrong side of the fabric.

- There should be no evidence of the bobbin thread on the right side of the fabric.

- The stitches should be smooth and regular, and the fabric should be flat and free of puckers.

TIP : Always stitch a test sample using the exact threads, needle, fabric, stitch pattern, and stabilizer you will be using in a project.

TIP : Always stitch a test sample after changing needles, threads, stitch pattern, fabric weight, or tension settings.

Needle Tension

On most machines, there is a tension dial with numbers ranging from 0 (no tension) to 10 (tightest tension). On other machines, the range is from – (minus; little tension) to + (plus; tightest tension). Normal sewing tension is the midpoint on the tension dial and is usually indicated. A setting of 4.5 to 5 is normal sewing tension for most machines. Often loosening the top tension is all that is required for forming good quality decorative stitches. Begin by adjusting the needle thread tension or top tension. Loosen the needle tension to at least 3. Stitch the first exercise in the book. If bobbin thread still shows on the right side of the fabric, then lower the needle tension more and test stitch. If adjusting the needle tension does not produce good quality decorative stitches, the bobbin tension will have to be adjusted.

NOTE: Using fine bobbin thread without loosening the needle tension often results in dots or "beads" of the white bobbin thread showing on the right side of the fabric. This is usually an undesired look.

Bobbin Tension

For regular sewing, normal bobbin tension is satisfactory. The fine bobbin threads used for machine embroidery, however, may require tightening of the bobbin tension. They are so thin, they slip through the bobbin tension spring much more easily than regular sewing thread. If reducing the needle tension does not produce good quality decorative stitches, the bobbin tension will have to be adjusted.

NOTE: While working through the exercises, if you alter bobbin tension, remember to make a note of any alterations on the machine set-up charts.

There are two types of bobbin assemblies: machines with removable bobbin cases, such as Bernina, Pfaff, and most Vikings; and machines with drop-in bobbins, such as Elna, Janome, and New Home. Follow the directions in your machine manual to adjust the bobbin tension. More general information for the two types of bobbin assemblies is given below.

TIP : No matter what type of machine you have, wind the bobbin thread slowly.

TIP : If the bobbin thread should show on the right side of the base fabric after loosening the needle and bobbin tensions, use a polyester thread that matches either the base fabric or the needle thread in the bobbin.

Machines with Removable Bobbin Cases

First, wind a bobbin with bobbin thread; wind this thread slowly. Remove the bobbin case from the machine. Hold the case so that the bobbin would fall out to the right. Locate the tension screw on the bobbin case. It is usually the larger of two screws. Turn the screw to the right to tighten the tension. ("Righty Tighty, Lefty Loosey!") Turn the screw ¼ to ½ turn at a time. Test the bobbin thread tension between turns.

To test the bobbin thread tension, insert the bobbin into the bobbin case and the bobbin thread through the tension band. Hold the case over your other hand so that you can catch it in case the tension is too loose or the bobbin comes out. Hold the end of the bobbin thread and gently shake the case once. The bobbin case should only move when you shake the thread. If the thread does not come out at all, loosen the tension. If the thread spools out quickly, tighten the tension.

Many machine embellishers purchase a second bobbin case, keeping one for regular sewing and using the second for decorative work. Mark the second case with a dot of colored nail polish and adjust the bobbin tension screw for fine bobbin thread, if needed. Your machine manual may make reference to setting the bobbin tension for decorative work.

TIP : Before you adjust the screw in the bobbin case, use an Ultra Fine Sharpie® marker to mark the screw's original position so you can reset it for normal sewing. Turn the screw slowly over a white terry cloth towel or piece of flannel. If the tiny screw comes out, it won't bounce out of sight.

TIP : It is helpful to have a second bobbin case so you do not have to repeatedly change the tension on the bobbin used for regular sewing.

☀ TIP : Always stitch a test sample after changing needles, threads, stitch pattern, or tension settings.

Machines with Drop-in Bobbins

We recommend that you adjust the bobbin tension only after exhausting all other options (loosening needle thread tension, changing bobbin thread, changing bobbin thread color). The tension setting on these machines can be difficult to regulate. First, wind a bobbin with bobbin thread; wind this thread slowly. Locate the tension screw. It's usually beside a scale similar to the scale for needle tension. Either mark the original bobbin setting or make a note of it. Tighten the tension by turning the screw towards the higher number or the plus sign, depending on the machine's marking system. You don't have to move the screw very much. Tug on the bobbin thread to test the tension. After some experience, you will know if the thread comes out too quickly. Again, refer to your manual or your machine dealer for help and suggestions.

Tension Test

Before you begin the exercises in this book, do a tension test. Begin with a piece of fabric labeled as shown in the diagram. Use a Ultra Fine Sharpie® Marker for best marking results. The numbers indicate tension settings.

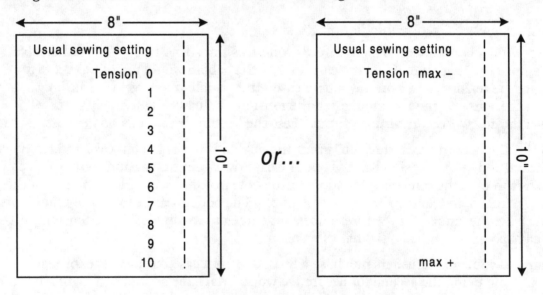

Set up the machine as follows:

Machine Set-up — Tension Test

Needle................. 90 / 14 embroidery
Thread .... metallic
Needle Tension .. variable
Stitch Name........ straight
Stitch Length...... 3
Stitch Width 0
Presser Foot........ appliqué, embroidery , satin stitch, or zig zag
Bobbin Thread ... fine bobbin thread

Begin stitching, leaving the machine at the tension setting used for normal sewing. As your row of stitching reaches the 0 mark on the fabric, reduce the tension to 0 or the lowest possible tension. Leaving your hand on the tension dial, gradually increase the tension to the setting number matching the number written on the fabric. When you have completed the row of stitching, remove the fabric from the machine, and examine the work from both the right and wrong sides. You will most likely see a marked difference between the loosest and tightest settings. The best tension for working with decorative threads results in the needle thread pulled slightly to the wrong side of the fabric. There should be no evidence of the bobbin thread on the right side of the fabric. The stitches should be smooth and regular, and the fabric should be flat and free of puckers. Depending on your machine, the tension setting may be slightly different for each decorative stitch you choose. Knowing how to do a tension test will help you determine the proper setting as you proceed with decorative work.

NOTE: While working through the exercises in this book, always do a tension test.

Learning the Techniques

The technique pages will help you explore the possibilities of embellishment with metallic threads and fibers. Each technique includes a description, a machine set-up chart, and stitch sample charts for you to fill in with the best settings for your machine.

Using the Machine Set-up Charts

Machine set-up charts accompany all of the techniques in this workbook. Not all charts include all of the elements shown here. Carefully following this set-up information should result in successful stitching.

⚜ Machine Set-up — Example

Needle.................. 90 / 14 embroidery
Thread .... metallic
Needle Tension .. 3
Stitch Name........ zig zag
Stitch Length...... 3
Stitch Width....... 3
Couching Fiber... 3 strands candlelight
Presser Foot........ cording, braiding, or couching
Bobbin Thread ... fine bobbin thread

Use these charts as a starting point. Because machines vary widely, you may get best results with slightly different settings. As you explore decorative threads, you will often alter the stitch length and / or width. In machine embellishment, there are few rules as long as the stitch quality is good. Let your own personal tastes and experiences be your guide.

⚜ TIP : You may have to change tension settings when you change stitch pattern, stitch length, stitch width, or thread.

Creating Your Stitch Journal

To get the most out of this book, we recommend you keep a stitch journal of your embellishment explorations. Keeping a journal is an easy and fun way to make your own reference guide. It can save you time and prevent frustration in the future as you incorporate these embellishment techniques in your projects.

To begin, we suggest you take this book to a good copy center. Remove the binding and punch three holes in the left margin of the pages. Put these pages in a large three ring binder. Add "top loading" plastic page protectors to your binder so you can insert your stitch samples in the page protectors next to the corresponding technique pages.

When you're ready to stitch, prepare your fabric as described on page 4. Slip an 8" x 10" piece of stabilizer between the wrong side of the fabric and needle plate. Stitch through the fabric and stabilizer.

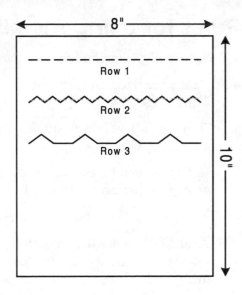

Make notes of thread color, stitch names / numbers, and machine settings (especially length, width, and tension) on the book pages and on the stitch samples using an Ultra Fine Sharpie® marker or Pigma Pen. You may also wish to number the stitch rows to correspond with the exercises. Store your stitch samples in the page protectors leaving the stabilizer in place for stiffness and durability. Record the most pleasing combinations on the exercise pages that accompany each technique. You will create your own personal embellishment reference guide that reflects your personal taste and the stitches of your own sewing machine.

Rules for Using Metallic Threads

- Sew slowly. Sewing fast can damage your machine and produce poor quality work.

- Match the needle to the thread you are using (see *Metallic Threads & Needles Chart*, page 43).

- Change your needle frequently when using metallic threads because they create a lot of friction, which is hard on the needle.

- Reduce needle thread tension. To loosen needle tension, move tension dial to a lower number on some machines; move to the minus range on other machines.

- Use fine bobbin thread in the bobbin and wind this thread very slowly.

- Clean & oil machine frequently, following the directions in your machine manual and the suggestions from above. Even a little piece of metallic thread in the bobbin area can cause sewing problems.

- Use stabilizer when doing decorative stitches to help support the fabric and the stitches. You can add more than one piece of stabilizer under the base fabric if you experience problems.

- Match the presser foot to the stitching and threads (see *Machine Accessory Feet*, page 4).

- Keep an eye on the needle spools as you sew. They may jerk during sewing and spin backwards a little, causing the thread to wrap around the spool pin. If this happens too often, try using a foam spool ring such as *The Finishing Touch Spool Ring* or a thread stand such as *The Thread Pro™* and the *Thread Palette*. The *Spool Tool™* is also great for taming decorative threads, especially Sliver.

- If you have trouble with metallic thread fraying and breaking, use *Sewer's Aid* on the spool of thread. *Sewer's Aid* is a silicone lubricant that reduces friction and heat build-up. It's colorless and absorbs into the thread. Don't use it on the mylar threads, because the thread does not absorb it. Try *Lube-A-Thread* to apply liquid silicone to the thread before going through the needle's eye. Also try one of the thread stands mentioned above.

- It's okay to start collecting a thread stash. Having a lot of wonderful fibers around spurs creativity and can be very therapeutic. Refer to *Point Well Taken* for a complete, up-to-date list of the many threads and fibers that are available.

- The rule for using metallic threads is *experiment, experiment, experiment* to see what works best on your machine with your thread and your fabrics. When working on a project, always stitch a test sample using the exact materials you'll be using in your project. Always stitch a test sample after changing needles, threads, or tension settings.

- Use a *Perfect Sew Needle Threader and Needle Inserter* for threading the metallic threads. The mylar threads can be especially difficult to thread, as the thread tail curls up.

NOTE: Do not use *Sewer's Aid* on mylar threads.

Metallic Thread

You can achieve sparkling decorative effects by simply stitching with metallic thread. Rows of straight stitches brighten fabric, whether stitched in straight, curved, or intersecting rows. Don't overlook the possibilities of stitching multiple rows of zig zag stitches. Surprisingly, you can produce pleasing embellishments by using utility stitches with metallic threads. Some of our favorite utility stitches are the blind hem and honeycomb stitch. Of course, it's always fun to use decorative stitches with metallic thread. For the exercises below, choose open decorative stitches. An open decorative stitch is any decorative stitch that does not have any satin stitch elements. Some examples of open decorative stitches include feather, cross, blanket, or entredeux.

⚙ Machine Set-up — Metallic Thread

Needle................. 80 / 12 metallica or 90 / 14 embroidery

Thread .... solid, variegated, or gradated metallic

Presser Foot........ satin stitch, embroidery, or appliqué

Bobbin Thread ... fine bobbin thread

Straight stitch

Stitch #: _____

Row Number: _____

Needle Tension: _____

SL: _____

Zig Zag stitch

Stitch #: _____

Row Number: _____

Needle Tension: _____

SL: _____

SW: _____

Several rows of straight stitching in straight rows

Stitch #: _____

Row Number: _____

Needle Tension: _____

SL: _____

Several rows of straight stitching in curved, intersecting rows

Stitch #: _____

Row Number: _____

Needle Tension: _____

SL: _____

SW: _____

Several rows of zig zag stitch in curved, intersecting rows

Stitch #: _____

Row Number: _____

Needle Tension: _____

SL: _____

SW: _____

Blind hem stitch

Stitch #: _____

Row Number: _____

Needle Tension: _____

SL: _____

SW: _____

Honeycomb stitch

Stitch #: _____

Row Number: _____

Needle Tension: _____

SL: _____

SW: _____

Utility stitch

Stitch Name or #: _____

Row Number: _____

Needle Tension: _____

SL: _____

SW: _____

Utility stitch

Stitch Name or #: _____

Row Number: _____

Needle Tension: _____

SL: _____

SW: _____

Open decorative stitch

Stitch Name or #: _____

Row Number: _____

Needle Tension: _____

SL: _____

SW: _____

Open decorative stitch

Stitch Name or #: _____

Row Number: _____

Needle Tension: _____

SL: _____

SW: _____

Open decorative stitch

Stitch Name or #: _____

Row Number: _____

Needle Tension: _____

SL: _____

SW: _____

Satin Stitch

Satin stitch is formed using a zig zag stitch with a very short stitch length. There are decorative stitches that contain satin stitch elements in all or part of the pattern. These are called *closed decorative stitches*. They include many floral and geometric motifs, such as scallops, hearts, and leaves.

Since satin stitches tend to look "blotchy" when stitched with variegated and gradated threads, you may wish to use solid color threads for satin stitching. Stitching the variegated thread exercise below will give you a good example of the "blotchy" look.

⚙ Machine Set-up — Satin Stitch

Needle.................. 80 / 12 metallica or 90 / 14 embroidery
Thread .... metallic
Presser Foot .... satin stitch, embroidery, or appliqué
Bobbin Thread ... fine bobbin thread

Satin stitch, solid color metallic

Stitch Name or #: _____

Row Number: _____

Needle Tension: _____

SL: _____

SW: _____

Satin stitch, variegated / gradated color metallic

Stitch Name or #: _____

Row Number: _____

Needle Tension: _____

SL: _____

SW: _____

Closed decorative stitch, solid metallic

Stitch Name or #: _____

Row Number: _____

Needle Tension: _____

SL: _____

SW: _____

Closed decorative stitch, variegated / gradated metallic

Stitch Name or #: _____

Row Number: _____

Needle Tension: _____

SL: _____

SW: _____

Closed decorative stitch, variegated / gradated metallic

Stitch Name or #: _____

Row Number: _____

Needle Tension: _____

SL: _____

SW: _____

Mylar Thread

Mylar threads add a lot more sparkle than twisted metallic threads. Because they are flat and springy, they tend to lay just *above* the surface of the fabric, whereas twisted metallic threads tend to be more relaxed and lay *on* the fabric surface. Because mylar threads are flat, they do not fill in satin stitch patterns as fully as do other metallic threads. A row of satin stitches sewn with metallic thread has a satiny look, while satin stitches sewn with mylar thread have a rougher texture with the background fabric peeking through.

This highly reflective thread produces exceptional brilliance even when used with just a straight stitch. Mylar threads bring utility and decorative stitching alive with shimmery highlights.

TIP : You don't get the very best straight stitch quality with mylar thread because it is a <u>flat</u> thread.

TIP : It is best to sew mylar thread with a bobbin that's more than one quarter full.

Machine Set-up — Mylar

Needle.................. 75 / 11 embroidery or 80 / 12 universal
Thread .... mylar
Presser Foot .... satin stitch, decorative stitch, or appliqué
Bobbin Thread ... fine bobbin thread

Straight stitch

Stitch #: _____

Row Number: _____

Needle Tension: _____

SL: _____

Satin stitch

Stitch #: _____

Row Number: _____

Needle Tension: _____

SL: _____

SW: _____

Overlock utility stitch

Stitch #: _____

Row Number: _____

Needle Tension: _____

SL: _____

SW: _____

Decorative stitch

Stitch name or #: _____

Row Number: _____

Needle Tension: _____

SL: _____

SW: _____

Star shape

Stitch Name or #: straight

Sample Number: _____

Needle Tension: _____

SL: _____

Utility stitch

Stitch #: _____

Row Number: _____

Needle Tension: _____

SL: _____

SW: _____

Decorative stitch

Stitch name or #: _____

Row Number: _____

Needle Tension: _____

SL: _____

SW: _____

Metallizing Printed Fabric

You can enhance printed fabrics by metallizing the design. You can add a little or a lot of sparkle by stitching over design elements with metallic threads. Stitching can be as basic as a straight stitch or a very narrow zig zag stitch. Decorative stitches can also highlight and embellish prints. The best patterns to highlight are those that allow for as much continuous stitching as possible. You don't have to limit metallizing to floral prints. Geometric prints, border prints, stripes, symmetrical and continuous patterns work well also. This technique is a great way to liven up dull or uninteresting fabrics. Choose either metallic or mylar thread depending on the print and your personal taste. Successful metallizing looks like the added embellishment was always there.

⚙ Machine Set-up — Metallizing Printed Fabric

Needle................. depends on thread selection, see chart, page 43
Thread .... metallic or mylar
Presser Foot........ satin stitch, decorative stitch, or appliqué
Bobbin Thread ... fine bobbin thread

Straight stitch

Thread: _____

Stitch #: _____

Sample Number: _____

Needle Tension: _____

SL: _____

SW: _____

Decorative stitch

Thread: _____

Stitch name or #: _____

Sample Number: _____

Needle Tension: _____

SL: _____

SW: _____

Narrow zig zag

Thread: _____

Stitch #: _____

Sample Number: _____

Needle Tension: _____

SL: _____

SW: _____

General Information About Couching

Couching is an easy technique for using threads, fibers, and trims that are too large to go through the needle eye. Simply machine stitch over the thicker threads and trims to anchor them to the base fabric. Couching gives great embellishment effects in a little time. It requires very little practice to be able to use it successfully in a project. A presser foot grooved on the underside glides easily over heavier fibers while guiding them in place. Suitable presser feet include appliqué, braiding, cording, couching, embroidery, open-toe, piping, and ribbon feet. Match the thickness of the couching fibers to the depth of the foot groove. You may want to use a couching foot with a braiding guide to hold the yarn straight in front of the presser foot.

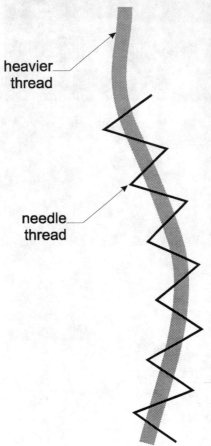

heavier
thread

needle
thread

For the needle thread, select regular sewing, decorative, or monofilament thread. Choose this thread based on the effect of the total design. Couching with a thread that matches the base fabric will allow the couched fiber to dominate the design. Stitching with a decorative thread can enhance the overall effect of the couching fiber. Monofilament thread is nearly invisible, and is a good choice for couching heavier fibers.

Use a zigzag or decorative stitch just wide enough to cross over the fibers without piercing them. If the bobbin thread should show on the right side of the base fabric after loosening the needle thread tension, use a polyester thread that matches the base fabric in the bobbin.

The following seven techniques and corresponding exercises expand on the many possibilities that couching offers.

☕ Machine Set-up — Couching

Needle.................. depends on thread, see chart, page 43

Thread .... metallic or mylar

Needle Tension .. 3

Stitch Name........ zig zag

Presser Foot .... cording, braiding, or couching

Bobbin Thread ... fine bobbin thread

Couching

Row Number: _____

Needle Thread: _____

Fiber: _____

Needle Tension: _____

SL: _____

SW: _____

Couching

Row Number: _____

Needle Thread: _____

Fiber: _____

Needle Tension: _____

SL: _____

SW: _____

Couching

Row Number: _____

Needle Thread: _____

Fiber: _____

Needle Tension: _____

SL: _____

SW: _____

Couching

Row Number: _____

Needle Thread: _____

Fiber: _____

Needle Tension: _____

SL: _____

SW: _____

Couching

Row Number: _____

Needle Thread: _____

Fiber: _____

Needle Tension: _____

SL: _____

SW: _____

Couching

Row Number: _____

Needle Thread: _____

Fiber: _____

Needle Tension: _____

SL: _____

SW: _____

Creating Couched Braid

Couching several strands of thin fibers with decorative threads creates a couched braid. A special machine foot called a cording foot has several holes or grooves that hold the fibers in place for couching. These feet can accommodate from three to nine fibers at a time. By using a variety of fiber textures and colors, as well as varying the needle thread, there are almost an infinite number of possible embellishment possibilities. These braids can form passementerie designs, couch down appliqué shapes, and embellish garments.

To stitch samples of couched braid, begin by selecting several fibers and a coordinating needle thread color. Match the thickness of the fiber to the size of the guide hole in the presser foot. Experiment to see if it is easier to thread the couching fibers in the braiding foot before or after attaching the foot to the machine. Do whichever is easier for you with your machine. You do not have to thread all the holes or grooves. Try different combinations of fibers to see the resulting braid designs. Also leave a long enough tail to the back of the foot to allow you to keep a good grasp of the fibers as you begin stitching.

The stitch that works best is one that has several steps such as the triple step zig zag stitch. This stitch takes three stitches to form the "zig" and three more stitches to form the "zag." Test stitch with the fibers as some fibers resist piercing by the needle and split or shred. Also check the width of the zig zag stitch; it needs to be wide enough to clear the outer fibers in the braid and securely anchor them to the fabric.

There are utility and open decorative stitches that you may also like for creating couched braid, depending on your project. Some of our favorites include the star stitch that looks like an asterisk, cross stitches, and the ladder stitch.

When you stitch, you can achieve gentle curves, but sharp curves and angles take practice. Experiment with different fibers, threads, and stitches to find the possibilities that please and interest you.

NOTE: Stitches that use triple motion (to back and forth and side to side to complete one part of the stitch) can be difficult to use with this technique as the braid fibers must move back and forth through the presser foot several times.

TIP : If you have trouble threading the cording foot, use a thin, blue Berol® dental floss threader, to guide the fibers through the holes or grooves. These threaders are found in the dental section of the drug store.

TIP : Draw passementerie patterns on Sulky Solvy for an easy-to-follow stitching guide.

TIP : Use the Multiple Cording Guide for guiding the fibers as you create braid.

TIP : Use a small piece of tape to secure the threads in place.

Needle................. depends on thread, see chart, page 43

Thread............... sewing, metallic, or monofilament

Needle Tension .. normal for regular sewing and monofilament; 3 for metallic

Stitch Name........ zig zag

Presser Foot........ cording, braiding, or couching

Bobbin Thread ... depends on thread, see chart, page 43

Braid, triple-step zig zag

Row Number: _____

Needle Thread: _____

Fibers: _____

Needle Tension: _____

SL: _____

SW: _____

Braid, utility stitch

Stitch name or #: _____

Row Number: _____

Needle Thread: _____

Fibers: _____

Needle Tension: _____

SL: _____

SW: _____

Braid, open decorative stitch

Stitch name or #: _____

Row Number: _____

Needle Thread: _____

Fibers: _____

Needle Tension: _____

SL: _____

SW: _____

Braid

Stitch name or #: _____

Row Number: _____

Needle Thread: _____

Fibers: _____

Needle Tension: _____

SL: _____

SW: _____

Braid

Stitch name or #: _____

Row Number: _____

Needle Thread: _____

Fibers: _____

Needle Tension: _____

SL: _____

SW: _____

Braid

Stitch name or #: _____

Row Number: _____

Needle Thread: _____

Fibers: _____

Needle Tension: _____

SL: _____

SW: _____

Braid

Stitch name or #: _____

Row Number: _____

Needle Thread: _____

Fibers: _____

Needle Tension: _____

SL: _____

SW: _____

Braid

Stitch name or #: _____

Row Number: _____

Needle Thread: _____

Fibers: _____

Needle Tension: _____

SL: _____

SW: _____

Braid

Stitch name or #: _____

Row Number: _____

Needle Thread: _____

Fibers: _____

Needle Tension: _____

SL: _____

SW: _____

Couching Twisted Fibers

Couching several strands of fibers that are twisted together creates a blend of colors and textures. Twisting several fibers together such as ribbon floss, candlelight, or bouclé, produces a thicker and often stronger couching fiber. Twisting several different strands also provides the opportunity to create unique color coordinated couching fibers. A special machine foot called a cording foot has a deep channel that accommodates thicker fibers and holds them in place for stitching. You may also use the *Pearls & Piping* ™ foot. Decorative needle threads add more options for creating this form of couched embellishment.

There are several tools for twisting fibers together. *On the Surface* and *Clotilde* sell the *Spinster* and *Lacis* has a *Thread Twirler*. Both of these tools are designed specifically for twisting fibers together. On some sewing machines you can use the bobbin winding spindle to twist fibers together. Tie the fiber ends through a hole of an empty bobbin (not the center hole). Then place the bobbin on the winding spindle. Be sure to run the bobbin winding motor slowly.

You can also use an egg beater or hand drill to twist fibers. If you remove the bit from a drill and replace it with a cup hook, you can attach knotted fiber ends over the hook.

To create the twisted fibers, use any of the tools or methods above and attach one end of the fibers to the tool. Tie the other end to a doorknob, a drawer handle, to a sewing bird, or have someone hold the ends. Hold the fibers slightly taut while twisting. Twist the fibers until they start to twist back on themselves. Then pinch the fibers in the middle and allow the ends to twist together.

To stitch samples of couched twisted fibers, begin by selecting several fibers and a coordinating needle thread. Twist together fibers that are long enough to ensure complete coverage of the embellishment path. Usually this length is about three to four times the distance the couching will cover.

Check to make sure the machine foot will accommodate the thickness of the twisted fibers. Also, leave a long enough tail at the back of the foot to allow you to keep a good grasp of the fibers as you begin stitching.

The stitch that works best to couch down twisted fibers is a zig zag stitch. Check the swing of the zig zag stitch to make sure it is wide enough to clear the outer fibers and securely anchor them to the fabric.

When you stitch, you can follow gentle curves, but sharp curves and angles take practice. Experiment with different fibers, threads, and presser feet to find the possibilities that please and interest you.

TIP : Because ribbon floss is a weak fiber, you can strengthen and protect it from fraying by twisting it with other fibers.

TIP : If you have trouble threading the cording foot, use a thin, blue Berol® dental floss threader to guide the fibers through the holes or grooves. These threaders are found in the dental section of the drug store.

Needle.................. depends on thread, see chart, page 43

Thread .... sewing, metallic, or monofilament

Needle Tension .. normal for regular sewing and monofilament; 3 for metallic

Stitch Name........ zig zag

Presser Foot .... cording, braiding, couching, or *Pearls & Piping*™

Bobbin Thread ... depends on thread, see chart, page 43

Twisted fibers

Row Number: _____

Needle: _____

Needle thread: _____

Fibers: _____

Needle Tension: _____

SL: _____

SW: _____

Twisted fibers

Row Number: _____

Needle: _____

Needle thread: _____

Fibers: _____

Needle Tension: _____

SL: _____

SW: _____

Twisted fibers

Row Number: _____

Needle: _____

Needle thread: _____

Fibers: _____

Needle Tension: _____

SL: _____

SW: _____

Twisted fibers

Row Number: _____

Needle: _____

Needle thread: _____

Fibers: _____

Needle Tension: _____

SL: _____

SW: _____

Twisted fibers

Row Number: _____

Needle: _____

Needle thread: _____

Fibers: _____

Needle Tension: _____

SL: _____

SW: _____

Twisted fibers

Row Number: _____

Needle: _____

Needle thread: _____

Fibers: _____

Needle Tension: _____

SL: _____

SW: _____

Twisted fibers

Row Number: _____

Needle: _____

Needle thread: _____

Fibers: _____

Needle Tension: _____

SL: _____

SW: _____

Twisted fibers

Row Number: _____

Needle: _____

Needle thread: _____

Fibers: _____

Needle Tension: _____

SL: _____

SW: _____

Twisted fibers

Row Number: _____

Needle: _____

Needle thread: _____

Fibers: _____

Needle Tension: _____

SL: _____

SW: _____

Braided Chain

Crossing a fiber while couching produces a couched chain. Couching a fine fiber, such as pearl cotton, results in a very dainty chain. Likewise, couching a heavier fiber, such as chenille yarn or Radiance, yields a bit thicker chain. Twisted fibers work well as couching fibers for this technique. Depending on the type of fiber, this embellishment can range from soft and delicate to glitzy or sporty. This is not a "zippy" technique, but it is a very effective embellishment.

To stitch samples of couched chain, plan and lightly mark the embellishment line. Cut the couching fiber twice the length of the embellishment line plus several inches. Allow more length for thicker fibers. It is much better to trim off excess fibers when finished than to run short of fibers and be unable to finish. Divide the couching fiber in half. Place the midpoint of the couching fiber at the beginning of the embellishment line.

If possible, set the needle to stop in the down position. Stitch over the couching fiber and backtack to anchor the end securely. Stitch two or more stitches. Raise the presser foot. Crisscross the couching fiber in front of the needle. Lower the presser foot. Take two stitches and raise the foot. Crisscross the couching fiber and stitch. Repeat to the end of the embellishment line. If you can program your machine, set the program for two straight stitches. The machine will automatically stop after taking two stitches. Otherwise, count stitches and stop with the needle in the fabric. Thin fibers require a short distance between crossings (⅜ inch); heavier fibers require a longer distance (½ inch). Try several different stitch lengths to see which works best for your fiber selection. Stick with the number of stitches you like best.

For a corded look, use very thin ribbon, braid, soutache, or couching fiber. Cut and anchor the trim as above. Cross the end in front of the needle then stitch over the crossed trim using three or more stitches. The thickness of the trim will determine the number of stitches needed to stitch across the trim. Repeat crossing the trim and stitching it down. Keep the trim from the left on top when crossing.

It is important to keep the tension on the couching fiber the same, thus keeping the size of the "chain links" consistent. With large couching fibers, you may need to increase the stitch length or take more stitches between crisscrosses. For the best look, be consistent in the number of stitches taken and in the tension on the fiber.

🪡 Machine Set-up — Braided Chain

Needle.................. depends on thread, see chart, page 43

Thread................ sewing, metallic, or monofilament

Needle Tension .. normal for regular sewing and monofilament; 3 for metallic

Stitch Name........ straight

Presser Foot........ satin stitch

Bobbin Thread ... depends on needle thread, see chart, page 43

Braided perle cotton

Row Number: _____

Needle: _____

Needle thread: _____

Needle Tension: _____

SL: _____

Bobbin thread: _____

Braided fiber

Row Number: _____

Needle: _____

Needle thread: _____

Fiber: _____

Needle Tension: _____

SL: _____

Bobbin thread: _____

Braided combination of twisted fibers

Row Number: _____

Needle: _____

Needle thread: _____

Fibers: _____

Needle Tension: _____

SL: _____

Bobbin thread: _____

Braided cord

Row Number: _____

Needle: _____

Needle thread: _____

Fiber: _____

Needle Tension: _____

SL: _____

Bobbin thread: _____

Special Couching Effects

Beads, cording, sequins, and rhinestones add special couching effects. Couching these trims poses some problems, but there are unique machine feet that aid in couching over these bulky and rigid trims. These machine feet have a deep channel that passes smoothly over these trims. Choose a *Pearls & Piping*™, *Sequins & Ribbon*™, or braiding foot. When selecting beads, cording, sequins, or rhinestones for couching, match their size to the channel on the machine foot. Select beads that are cross-locked because they will not slip off the end of the strand, melt under the iron, or come apart if a thread breaks.

Use a strong nylon monofilament thread in the needle to couch beads, sequins, and rhinestones without taking away from their special embellishment effects. Use a polyester or nylon thread in the bobbin. Before stitching, check the width of the zig zag stitch to ensure that the needle clears each side of the trim.

TIP : Bernina owners use the 21C foot to couch beads. This foot is specifically for the 1630 machine, but it can be used on other models as well.

Machine Set-up — Special Couching Effects

Needle................. 80 / 12 universal
Thread .... monofilament
Needle Tension .. normal sewing
Stitch Name........ zig zag
Bobbin Thread ... polyester sewing

Beads

Row Number: _____

Needle Tension: _____

SL: _____

SW: _____

Presser foot: *Pearls & Piping*™

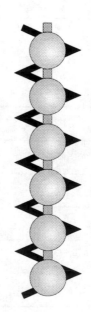

Cording

Row Number: _____

Needle Tension: _____

SL: _____

SW: _____

Presser foot: cording, *Pearls & Piping*™

Rhinestones

Row Number: _____

Needle Tension: _____

SL: _____

SW: _____

Presser foot: cording, *Pearls & Piping*™

Sequins

Row Number: _____

Needle Tension: _____

SL: _____

SW: _____

Presser foot: *Sequins & Ribbon* ™

Couching Ribbons and Fabric Strips

Couching ribbons and fabric strips using decorative threads and stitch patterns provides a unique and fun way to embellish. The resulting effect is similar to making decorative braid with ribbon. Choose a ribbon that is about ½" wide and cut it a little longer than the base fabric. Use an appliqué foot or *Sequins & Ribbon Foot*™ to hold the ribbon flat for easy couching. Choose a coordinating decorative thread and an open decorative or utility stitch. Stitch the ribbon in place or embellish the ribbon as you stitch it into place on the base fabric.

Create a new embellished fabric by couching many fabric strips to a base fabric. Cut or tear fabric into strips a little longer than the base fabric and in a variety of widths from ½" to ¾" wide. Mark a few parallel lines on the base fabric in order to line up the fabric strips. Keep the strips parallel and close to each other. Allow some background fabric to peek from between the strips. Use several rows of stitching to couch down the fabric strips. Vary the decorative thread colors as well as the stitch patterns. The resulting fabric will be a blend of color, pattern, and texture.

TIP : Add strips of Ultrasuede® or Ultrasuede Light® to vary the texture of the strips.

TIP : Using fabric strips for couching is a good way to use up scraps.

Machine Set-up — Couching Ribbons & Fabric Strips

Needle................. depends on thread, see chart, page 43
Thread .... decorative thread
Needle Tension .. 3
Bobbin Thread ... fine bobbin thread

Couched ribbon

Stitch name or #: _____

Row Number: _____

Needle: _____

Thread: _____

Needle Tension: _____

SL: _____

SW: _____

Presser foot: appliqué or *Sequins & Ribbon Foot*™

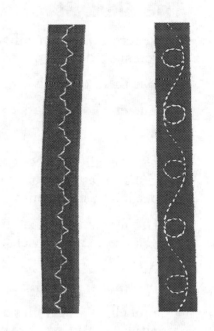

Couched fabric strips

Stitch name or #: _____

Row Number: _____

Needle: _____

Thread: _____

Needle Tension: _____

SL: _____

SW: _____

Presser foot: satin or appliqué

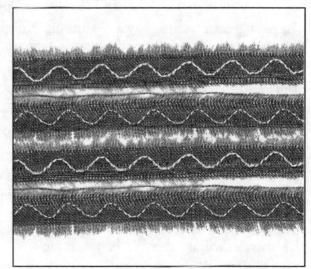

The Next Step: Using These Techniques in a Project

These techniques can enhance many of your sewing projects. Here are some ideas to get you started:

- Use them on ready-to-wear, purchased accessories, gift items, and linens.

- Add embellishments to collars, cuffs, or front bands.

- Add braided chains to give special touches to baby layette items and fine lingerie.

- Use metallized pieces of fabric for collars, yolks, cuffs, quilt pieces, or as "whole cloth" or as the fabric you've created for pillow tops, tote bags, wall hangings, decorative accessories, etc.

- Use any of these techniques in home decorating projects such as pillows, borders on valances, and tie backs.

- Add embellishments to sheet hems, pillow cases, guest towels, dinner napkins, placemats, cocktail napkins, table runners, and holiday linens.

- Embellish accessories and gift items such as totes, chatelaine ribbons, sewing kits, gift bags, and eyeglass cases.

- Enhance a quilted wall hanging with metallic quilting.

- Add your own special signature look to your quilt label.

These suggestions are only a beginning. Embellishment gives you an opportunity to show your creative side and give your own personal signature to your projects.

Securing and Hiding Fiber Ends

There are several methods for securing fiber ends. Choose the option that fits the fiber, the embellishment design, and the base fabric. It is important to plan the securing method when planning the whole design.

The easiest method is to simply begin and end couching in seam allowances. The seam will secure and hide fiber tails. A good method for securing and hiding thick yarns or cord is to cover the ends with satin stitching. After completing the couching, cover the fiber tails at the beginning and ending points. Choose a decorative thread that fits into the overall design. It could be the same color as the couched fiber or another color that coordinates with the embellishment. Stitch over the fibers beginning about ½" from the raw ends. Gradually reduce the stitch width so the stitches form a wedge or triangle shape. The satin stitches should cover all the couched strands.

Additionally, you can conceal the ends inside folds or pleats of the base fabric. Or, place an appliqué over the ends of the couched fibers. Using fabric to hide the fiber ends incorporates couching with other embellishment or manipulation techniques.

For finer fibers, you can tuck under the raw edges and couch them down. Fold under about ½" of fiber at the beginning and ending points. Couch over this double thickness to hide the raw edges.

For finer fibers you can also draw the fiber tails to the wrong side of the base fabric. Leave a thread and fiber tail that is at least 6" long at the beginning and ending points. Thread the tails through the eye of a crewel needle or any needle with a large eye and a sharp point. Insert the needle into the base fabric just beyond the point where the

---

machine stitching begins. Draw the tails to the wrong side. Tie the tails. Do the same at the end of the couching. Carefully apply a dot of seam sealant and allow to dry.

For a casual look, leave long fiber tails on the right side of the fabric. You can tie a knot to secure, and slip beads, charms, shells, or other embellishments on the tails. This securing technique extends the use of the fibers for embellishment and needs to fit the overall design of the project.

Glossary

These products and terms are defined more completely in *Point Well Taken*.

appliqué / embroidery / satin stitch or zig zag foot

This foot has a groove on the bottom to accommodate a heavy build-up of wide satin and decorative stitches. Some appliqué feet have "open toes" or are clear, giving a good view of the stitching path.

braid

Braid is created by couching several strands of fibers side by side. See page 26.

braiding / couching / cording

This foot has either one large hole and deep groove for couching one thick fiber or the foot has several holes or grooves for couching several fibers at once.

braiding guide

This wire guide is used in conjunction with a cording foot and attaches to the back of the foot. It keeps one fiber or a twist of fibers in place in front of the foot. This accessory is made by *Husquvarna Viking*.

closed decorative stitches

Any decorative stitch that has satin stitch elements in all or part of a pattern is a closed decorative stitch. Sometimes, closed decorative stitches are referred to as compact stitches. Many floral and geometric motifs have satin stitch elements. Some examples of closed decorative stitches include scallop, heart, leaf. See page 15.

couching

See page 24.

couching fibers

These fibers are heavier threads that can not go through the eye of the needle. See page 24.

embroidery / metallic needles

These needles are designed for trouble-free sewing with decorative threads. The needles have several improvements and modifications to reduce skipped stitches, damaged fabric, and frayed thread. See page 6.

exercise

Stitching of a specific stitch, pattern, or set of stitches using the suggested machine set-up chart.

lingerie or bobbin thread

This thread is a fine weight thread for use in the needle in heirloom sewing or for use in the bobbin when stitching with decorative threads. Some examples include *YLI Lingerie & Bobbin Thread* and *Sulky Bobbin* thread. See page 6.

metallic thread

This decorative thread is a combination of fibers and metal that add sparkle to stitches. Avoid metallics that are stiff, fray badly, or have a lot of the white core fiber showing. See page 15.

metallizing

Metallizing is an embellishment technique of adding decorative details and highlights to a printed fabric with metallic threads. See page 22.

monofilament thread

This soft, translucent thread that comes in clear and smoke. Use this thread when you want the stitching to be invisible. We use the smoke color more often.

multiple cording guide

This plastic guide has five holes to keep embroidery threads lined up where you want them. This guide keeps the fibers from being twisted and tangled. It is used with a cording foot that can accommodate several separate fibers.

mylar thread

This decorative thread is a flat, ribbon-like decorative thread such as *Sulky Sliver*. See page 20.

open decorative stitch

A decorative stitch that does not have any satin stitch elements is an open decorative stitch. Some examples include feather, cross, blanket, or entreaueux. See page 15.

passementerie

This clothing embellishment technique is created with heavier trims and cords couched down into a design or pattern.

Pearls & Piping™

This foot is manufactured by *Creative Feet™* and has a deep channel for cording heavier decorative fibers, beads, and rhinestones up to ¼' in thickness.

satin stitch

Satin stitch is a zig zag stitch sewn with a very short stitch length (0.5) See page 18.

Sequins & Ribbon™

This foot is manufactured by *Creative Feet™* and has adjustable guides and open toe for couching ribbons and sequins.

silicone

This product is a liquid used to reduce friction, heat build-up, and fraying of decorative threads. See page 14.

stabilizer

A sewing notion that provides necessary backing and support for embellishment stitching. See page 6. (For a complete list and more information on stabilizers, see *Point Well Taken*).

technique

A method of creating an embellishment.

3-Step zig zag stitch

This stitch takes three stitches to complete the "zig" and three stitches to complete the "zag."

utility stitch

One of several stitches designed for a particular garment construction or home dec. function. Some examples of utility stitches are zig zag, knit, overlock, blind hem, and edge stitch.

Supply Sources

If you can't find the supplies mentioned in this book at your local sewing machine dealer, quilt shop, specialty fabric shop, smocking shop, or heirloom sewing shop, check these great resources.

Please check around home first, as it's always better to support your local shops where you receive helpful advice and good customer service.

Clotilde, free notions catalog, *800-772-2891* or **http://www.clotilde.com**

In Cahoots, free pattern, book, & notions catalog, 800-95-CAHOOTS, or **http://www.in-cahoots.com**

Nancy's Notions, free notions catalog, *800-833-0690*

SCS, free catalog, *800-542-4727*

Sew Steady Portable Machine Table, call **Dream World,** *208-267-7136*

Sew-Art International, free catalog, *800-231-2787*

SpeedStitch, free catalog, *800-874-4115*

Summa Design, free catalog, *513-454-0943*

Threadline, free brochure, *800-237-4354*

ThreadPro, check with local Viking dealer or call Pamela Burke at *214-369-1614*

TreadleArt, catalog $ 3 (refundable with order), *310-534-5122*

The Weaving Edge, sample card $ 1.50 (refundable with order), *540-992-3497*

Web of Thread, free catalog, *502-575-9700*

In Cahoots® Metallic Thread and Needles Chart

Thread Selection	Needle Selection	Bobbin Thread
Metallic Thread (Sulky, Madeira, YLI, etc.)	Embroidery 80 / 12 – 90 / 14 or Metallic 80 / 12 or Metallica 80 / 12 or Topstitching 90 / 14	Fine bobbin thread
Madeira F/S Jewel	Embroidery 90 / 14 or Topstitching 90 / 14	Fine bobbin thread
Madeira Supertwist	Embroidery 90 / 14 or Topstitching 90 / 14	Fine bobbin thread
Sulky Sliver	Universal 80 / 12 or Embroidery 75 / 11 or Metallic 80 / 12 or Metallica 80 / 12	Fine bobbin thread
Madeira Jewel	Universal 80 / 12 or Embroidery 75 / 11 or Metallic 80 / 12 or Metallica 80 / 12	Fine bobbin thread
Prizm™ Hologram Thread	Universal 80 / 12 or Embroidery 75 / 11 or Metallic 80 / 12 or Metallica 80 / 12	Fine bobbin thread
Monofilament Thread	Universal 70 / 10 — 80 / 12	Fine bobbin thread or polyester sewing thread
Sewing Thread	Universal 70 / 10 — 80 / 12	Sewing thread

In Cahoots ®

Setting the new standard in wearable art patterns

All of our classroom-tested patterns and books feature incredibly thorough directions, detailed machine set-up charts, helpful diagrams, hints, and tips.

Mosaic Magic

The perfect first garment project!

This colorful adaptation of Seminole patchwork is rotary-cut and strip-pieced. If you are a quilter who has never sewn a garment before, or if you're just eager to work with lots of colorful fabrics, *Mosaic Magic* is a terrific project for you.. All you need are beginning sewing skills — most of the sewing is straight seams.

This pattern has incredibly thorough directions and helpful drawings. It includes directions for making quick and easy continuous bias binding.

This magic play of color, light, and texture is no sleight-of-hand!

Are you eager to learn embellishment and manipulation, but don't know where to begin? Then *Moonstruck* is *the* pattern for you.

Create your own fabrics and sew this flattering vest. Combine metallic threads, couching fibers, and specialty fabrics while learning five easy and fun embellishment techniques.

Moonstruck

Order now! Call 1-800-95-CAHOOTS (1-800-952-2466) or FAX 1-770-992-9678

Sheer Illusions

These eight embellishment techniques are sheer fun!

The soft hues of the *Sheer Illusions* palette create a pleasant flow of colors reminiscent of Impressionist paintings and colorwash quilts. Instead of using many small blocks of fabrics for color blending, *Sheer Illusions* creates watercolor effects by combining layers of sheer fabrics. This pastel palette is a classic for every woman.

Detailed machine setup directions for each technique and tips on bobbin work are included.

Wearable art has never been so classy... or so easy!

Express yourself with our unique weaving technique as you create a striking one-of-a-kind garment. You'll find creative new ways to combine colors and textures of fabric, ribbons, yarns, and trims.

Designed with a feminine style in mind, this soft and supple vest is versatile and great for travel. The *Easy Woven Vest* definitely has a designer look.

Pattern includes a SpeedWeaving™ needle and EasyWeave™ directions for better results in half the time! Incredibly thorough instructions and simple finishing methods help you make your fully-lined vest.

Easy Woven Vest

To help you be your creative best, all In Cahoots patterns include:

- Classroom-tested techniques and instructions
- Thorough machine set-up charts for each embellishment technique
- Accurate, step-by-step instructions for each technique
- Complete garment finishing instructions that teachers and students will love
- Complete supply lists
- Multi-sized from Small to Extra Extra Large

Order now! Call 1-800-95-CAHOOTS (1-800-952-2466) or FAX 1-770-992-9678

Great Squares

Create your own fabrics, then combine them to make the multi-colored, multi-patterned, and multi-textured Great Squares vest.

This pattern has seven different embellishment techniques and a new way to piece squares. Learn exciting ways to make pin tucks and pleats. You'll love the incredibly detailed instructions and drawings.

Great Squares includes a supplement for the embroidery machines and popular wool flannels, as well as valuable information about decorative threads and specialty needles. Detailed machine setup directions for each technique help beginners and experienced sewers.

Great Beginnings is your blueprint for vest success!

Create your own one-of-a-kind vest with our most versatile pattern! Display your patchwork, fabric manipulation, and embellishment skills. In Cahoots' *Great Beginnings* vest pattern covers all the construction details and lets you concentrate on creating your fabrics.

Terrific for teachers and intermediate to advanced sewers, it's the first pattern to provide you with incredibly thorough instructions, detailed drawings and supply list for:

- Four front design options combining five interchangeable pattern pieces
- Four finishing methods, including topstitching, reversible, bound, and piped
- Four back styles and two optional pocket designs

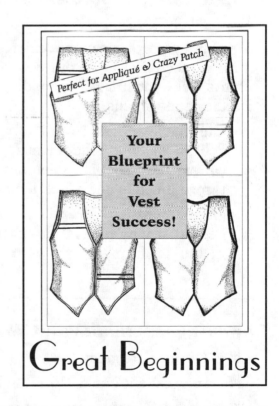

Perfect for Appliqué & Crazy Patch

Your Blueprint for Vest Success!

Great Beginnings

Our customers are saying...

- "It's just like having the teacher in your sewing room!"
- "The designs are flattering... the length is perfect!"
- "Great directions!"
- "I ordered one of your patterns, and it was so easy to follow that I have to order the rest!"

Order now! Call 1-800-95-CAHOOTS (1-800-952-2466) or FAX 1-770-992-9678

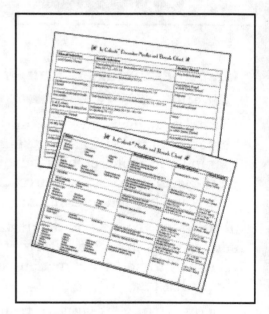

Check out our wonderful new embellishment workbooks!

Gourmet

Embellishments

with Metallic Threads & Fibers

An In Cahoots® embellishment workbook
by Debbie Garbers and Janet F. O'Brien

Get creative with **Gourmet Embellishments!**

- Twelve creative techniques
- Complete machine set-up information
- Essential information about couching
- Needles & Threads Chart for quick and easy reference
- Wonderful tips and hints to improve your use of metallic threads and fibers

Double your embellishment options!

- No fancy machine required... all you need is a front-threading zig-zag machine, and you'll be "twinning" in no time!
- Twelve techniques using twin needles and decorative threads
- Complete machine set-up information
- Twin needle chart for quick and easy reference
- Packed with tips and hints to help you get the most from decorative threads and twin needles

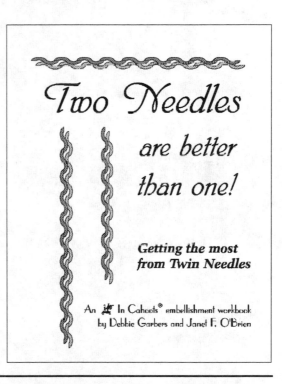

Two Needles are better than one!

Getting the most from Twin Needles

An In Cahoots® embellishment workbook
by Debbie Garbers and Janet F. O'Brien

Our machine set-up charts help you spend your time sewing... not fiddling!

Our easy-to-read charts, as shown here, are featured in these workbooks and in all of our embellished patterns.

Needle:	75 / 11 embroidery	*Stitch:*	honeycomb
Thread:	rayon	*SW:*	3
Tension:	3	*SL:*	3
Presser foot:	appliqué, embroidery, open toe, satin stitch, or zig zag	*Fine bobbin thread*	

Order now! Call 1-800-95-CAHOOTS (1-800-952-2466) or FAX 1-770-992-9678

In Cahoots Order Form

PO Box 72336
Marietta, GA 30007-2336
770-641-0945
FAX 770-992-9678

• 800-95-CAHOOTS (orders only)
• email: orders@in-cahoots.com
• web: http://www.in-cahoots.com

Date: _____

Name: _____

Address: _____

_____

City: _____ State: _____ Zip: _____

Phone: _____ FAX: _____

Item	Description	Price	Quantity	Amount
1017	Mosaic Magic Vest	$9.00		
1018	Easy Woven Vest	$10.00		
1019	Moonstruck Vest	$10.00		
1020	Great Squares Vest	$11.00		
1021	Great Beginnings Vest	$12.00		
1022	Sheer Illusions Vest	$12.00		
1101	Point Well Taken Book	$14.00		
1102	Gourmet Embellishments Book	$14.00		
1103	Two Needles are better than one! Book	$14.00		
1201	Laminated Sewing Chart	$4.00		
1202	Laminated Decorative Chart	$4.00		

Shipping Charges

First pattern .... $2.50   Each addt'l pattern or book $1.00
First book .... $3.00   Over $100 .... UPS charge

Subtotal _____
Shipping _____
Total _____

Customer signature: _____